DATE DUE

APR 0 2 2007		
MAR 0 2 2009		
MAY 2 5 2011		
MAR 2 9 2012		
MAY 2 0		
SEP 0 3 2013		

Demco, Inc. 38-293

Countries of the World

Israel

by Kristin Thoennes

Consultants:
Kim Cooper, Director of Special Projects
Merav Elkan, Director of Public Affairs
Consulate General of Israel to the Midwest

Bridgestone Books

an imprint of Capstone Press
Mankato, Minnesota

Bridgestone Books are published by Capstone Press
818 North Willow Street, Mankato, Minnesota 56001
http://www.capstone-press.com

Library of Congress Cataloging-in-Publication Data
Thoennes, Kristin.
   Israel/Kristin Thoennes.
   p. cm.—(Countries of the world)
   Summary: Discusses the history, landscape, people, animals, food, sports, and culture of Israel.
   ISBN 0-7368-0152-9
   1. Israel—Juvenile literature. [1. Israel.] I. Title. II. Series: Countries of the world (Mankato, Minn.)
   DS102.95.T56   1999
   956.94—dc21   98-33982
                                                                                   CIP
                                                                                    AC

Editorial Credits

Blanche R. Bolland, editor; Timothy Halldin, cover designer; Linda Clavel and Timothy Halldin, illustrators;
   Kimberly Danger and Sheri Gosewisch, photo researchers

Photo Credits

Jerry Ruff, 5 (bottom)
PhotoBank, Inc., 14
Photo Network, 6, 8
Photri-Microstock, 10, 18, 20
StockHaus Limited, 5 (top)
Unicorn Stock Photos/Jeff Greenberg, cover
Unicorn Stock Photos, 12
Valan Photos, 16

Table of Contents

Fast Facts

Name: State of Israel
Capital: Jerusalem
Population: About 5.5 million
Languages: Hebrew, Arabic, English
Religions: Judaism, Islam

Size: 7,876 square miles (20,399 square kilometers). *Israel is about the same size as the U.S. state of New Jersey.*
Crops: Oranges, olives, grapes

Maps

4

Flag

Israel's flag is white with a blue, six-pointed star in the center. The Star of David stands for Judaism. Israel is the homeland of the Jewish people. A blue stripe runs across the top of the flag. Another blue stripe is near the bottom. The flag's colors are those of the Jewish prayer shawl. Jewish men wear this cloth when they pray. White means pure. Blue stands for the sky.

Currency

Israel's unit of currency is the new shekel. There are 100 agorots in a new shekel.

In the late 1990s, about 4.2 new shekels equaled 1 U.S. dollar. About 2.7 new shekels equaled 1 Canadian dollar.

The Land

Israel is a small country in the Middle East. This region connects Africa and Asia. Israel became a country on May 14, 1948. Before this date, the land was called Palestine. Much of the land was a bare desert in 1948.

Israel has several types of land. A plain lies along the Mediterranean coast. Northern Israel has many mountains. Hills and valleys cover much of central Israel. The large Negev Desert lies in the south.

Israel's Dead Sea is the lowest place on earth. The water in the Dead Sea contains eight times as much salt as most seawater. Fish and plants cannot live in the Dead Sea.

Israel receives little rain. The lack of rain creates a water shortage throughout Israel. Israelis must irrigate much of their country. Pipes bring water to crops from far away.

Most of the land in Israel is dry.

The People

Israel is the only country in which most people are Jewish. The word Jewish describes a culture and a religion. Culture means the way people live and what they believe. The religion of Jewish people is called Judaism. Most Israeli Jews speak Hebrew.

Other Israelis are Arabs. They speak Arabic. Most Arabs practice the religion of Islam. They are called Muslims. Some Arabs are Christian.

Men in Israel sometimes wear special head coverings. Jewish men and boys might wear a kipah (ki-PAH). These small caps fit close to the head. Many older Arab men wear a long head covering called a kaffiyeh (kah-FEE-yeh).

Jerusalem is a holy city for Jews, Muslims, and Christians. Jerusalem's Western Wall is the remains of an old Jewish temple. The Dome of the Rock marks a historical site for Muslims. Christians believe Jesus died on a cross in Jerusalem.

Jerusalem is a holy city for three major religions.

Life at Home

Nearly 90 percent of Israelis live in cities. Most of these Israelis own apartments.

Israelis often use the sun to heat their water. Flat collectors on roofs trap the sun's energy. This energy then heats water stored inside buildings.

Some Bedouin Arabs live in tents in the desert. They raise sheep, goats, and camels. Bedouins move from place to place to find grass and water for their animals.

A kibbutz (kee-BOOTS) is a community in which members share everything. Each person has a job to do. No one gets paid. Instead, members receive food, houses, education, and care.

Another type of Israeli community is the moshav (moh-SHAHV). Each family in a moshav owns land and a house. The families combine their crops and sell them together. They then use the money to buy supplies.

Many kibbutzim are farming communities.

Going to School

Israeli children attend school from ages 5 to 18. All children go to kindergarten. Students then go to grade school for six years. They attend junior high school for three years. High school also lasts three years. Classes usually meet six days a week.

Jewish and Arab children attend different schools. But they learn the same lessons. Teachers in Jewish schools give lessons in Hebrew. Arab students learn their lessons in Arabic. Special schools move around with Bedouin Arabs.

Israeli children study many subjects. All students begin to learn English in the fourth grade. They take history, math, and science classes. Students also learn about farming and machinery. They can take art and music lessons.

Jewish Israeli children have classes in Hebrew.

Israeli Food

Spicy foods are popular in Israel. Many people eat a flat bread sandwich called a falafel (fuh-LAH-fel). Fried balls of vegetables with spices fill the pockets of the flat bread. Israelis often buy falafels at street stands.

Hummus (HOH-mus) is another spicy food. Hummus is a paste of mashed chickpeas, lemon, and garlic. Israelis put hummus on flat bread or use it as a dip.

Israelis eat a wide variety of dairy foods, fruits, and vegetables. Yogurt is especially popular. Many citrus fruits grow in Israel. Oranges and tangerines are most common.

Some Israelis eat only kosher (KOH-sher) food. Jewish law says kosher food is correct to eat. Jews who follow this law cannot have milk and meat at the same meal. They also cannot eat pork and some seafood.

Falafels are a popular food in Israel.

Animals and Plants

More than 380 types of birds live in Israel. Pelicans, herons, and storks nest near the Mediterranean Sea. Eagles, vultures, and hawks make their homes in the mountains.

Reptiles thrive in Israel's hot, dry weather. About 75 types of lizards and snakes live in the Negev Desert. Chameleons and agama lizards are native to Israel.

Some larger animals also live in Israel. Mountain gazelles graze in the hills. Foxes and leopards make their homes in wooded areas.

Many animals that once lived in Israel have disappeared. A wildlife program works to bring animals to Israel. Laws now protect the animals.

Prickly pear cactuses grow on the Negev Desert. The Hebrew name for their fruit is Sabra. A Sabra is tough on the outside but sweet inside. A person born in Israel also is called a Sabra.

Chameleons change color to match their surroundings.

Sports and Games

Soccer and basketball are the most popular sports in Israel. Israel's teams play around the world. Many Israelis enjoy watching ball games on television.

Hiking and swimming also are popular in Israel. Many Israelis hike in large groups. Some favor the hills near Jerusalem for hiking. Others like to hike in the desert. Israelis of all ages join in a special swimming event every year. They swim the three miles across the Sea of Galilee.

Jewish athletes from around the world play in the Maccabiah (mah-KAH-bee-yah) Games. This sporting event takes place in Israel every four years. The Maccabiah Games also celebrate Jewish culture.

Many Israelis play backgammon and chess. These board games require thinking of plans to move the pieces.

Many Israelis hike in large groups.

Holidays

Israeli Jews observe two important holidays in the fall. Rosh Hashanah (ROHSH hah-shah-NAH) marks the start of the Jewish New Year. Jews do not eat or drink on Yom Kippur (YOM kip-OOR). They pray for forgiveness for what they have done wrong in the last year.

Muslims celebrate Ramadan in the fall. They eat only at night for a month. They then celebrate by eating sweet pastries.

Purim and Pesach (PAY-sahk) are spring holidays. Jews celebrate Purim with carnivals and parades. During the week of Pesach, Jews celebrate their freedom.

Israelis celebrate two national holidays in the spring. On Memorial Day, they remember people who died for their country. The next day is Independence Day. People celebrate the creation of Israel with parades and dances.

Children wear costumes to celebrate Purim.

Hands On: Dance the Hora

The hora (ho-RAH) is Israel's most popular folk dance. Israelis dance the hora on Independence Day and at many other celebrations. You can dance the hora alone or in a group.

What You Need

Any number of dancers
Music with two beats in each measure

What You Do

1. Step to the left with your left foot.
2. Put your right foot behind your left.
3. Step to the left with your left foot.
4. Hop once on your left foot. Swing your right foot in front of your left.
5. Hop once on your right foot. Swing your left foot in front of your right.
6. Repeat steps 1-5 until the music stops.

Learn to Speak Hebrew

father	aba	(AH-bah)
good-bye and		
hello and **peace**	shalom	(shah-LOHM)
mother	ima	(EE-mah)
no	lo	(LO)
please	bevakasha	(be-VAH-kah-sha)
thank you	toda	(toh-DAH)
yes	ken	(KEN)

Words to Know

Bedouin (BED-uh-win)—an Arab group that lives in tents; Bedouins often move from place to place.

kaffiyeh (kah-FEE-yeh)—cloth wrapped around the head and held with a cord; many Arab men wear a kaffiyeh.

kipah (ki-PAH)—a small, round cap that some Jewish men and boys wear, especially at religious services

kosher (KOH-sher)—food made according to Jewish religious laws

Read More

Allard, Denise. *Israel.* Austin, Texas: Raintree Steck-Vaughn, 1997.

Bickman, Connie. *Children of Israel.* Through the Eyes of Children. Edina, Minn.: Abdo & Daughters, 1994.

King, David C. *Dropping in on Israel.* Vero Beach, Fla.: Rourke Publications, 1995.

Useful Addresses and Internet Sites

Embassy of Israel
3514 International Drive NW
Washington, DC 20008

Embassy of Israel
1005-50 O'Connor
Ottawa, ON K1P 6L2
Canada

Israel Internet Guide
http://www.iGuide.co.il
Virtual Tour of Jerusalem
http://www.md.huji.ac.il/vjt

Index